# Hidden Pictures

*Whoosh*—these busy trains are zipping thr[ough]
There are 12 hidden objects in the scene. How [...]

waffle

wedge of lemon

doughnut

banana

domino

slice of pizza

crescent moon

ladder

artist's brush

toothbrush

ruler

comb

# Top Spot

**Wow**, this puzzle has us coming and going. We've hidden 23 palindromes—
words that are spelled the same forward and backward—in this grid.
Search for them up, down, across, and diagonally.

### Word List

| | | | | |
|---|---|---|---|---|
| ~~BIB~~ | DEWED | MOM | RADAR | SAGAS |
| CIVIC | KAYAK | NOON | REDDER | SEES |
| DAD | LEVEL | PEEP | REFER | SOLOS |
| DEED | MADAM | POP | REPAPER | TENET |
| | | RACECAR | ROTATOR | TOOT |

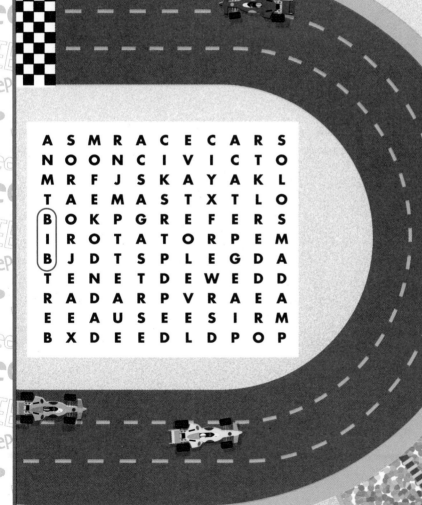

```
A S M R A C E C A R S
N O O N C I V I C T O
M R F J S K A Y A K L
T A E M A S T X T L O
B O K P G R E F E R S
I R O T A T O R P E M
B J D T S P L E G D A
T E N E T D E W E D D
R A D A R P V R A E A
E E A U S E E S I R M
B X D E E D L D P O P
```

# Tic Tac Boat

Each of these sailboats has something in common with the other two sailboats in the same row—across, down, and diagonally. For example, in the top row across, all three boats have two sails. Can you tell what's alike in each row?

# Loopy Language

**Can you match each language to its way of saying BOAT?**

1. _____ German
2. _____ Spanish
3. _____ Welsh
4. _____ Indonesian
5. _____ Hmong
6. _____ Swahili
7. _____ French

**A.** mashua
**B.** perahu
**C.** le bateau
**D.** das Boot
**E.** cwch
**F.** el barco
**G.** nkoj

Art by Robert Prince

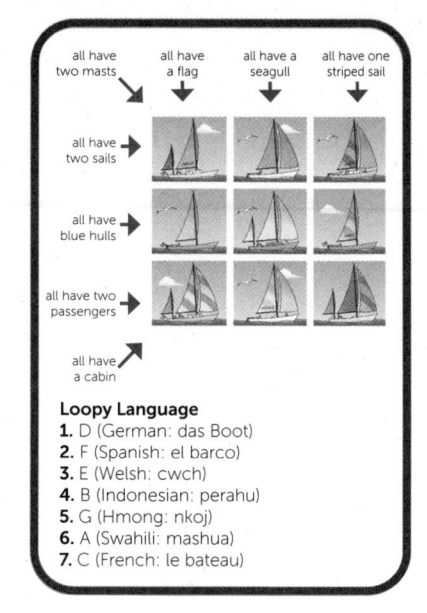

all have two masts    all have a flag    all have a seagull    all have one striped sail

all have two sails

all have blue hulls

all have two passengers

all have a cabin

## Loopy Language
**1.** D (German: das Boot)
**2.** F (Spanish: el barco)
**3.** E (Welsh: cwch)
**4.** B (Indonesian: perahu)
**5.** G (Hmong: nkoj)
**6.** A (Swahili: mashua)
**7.** C (French: le bateau)

# Field Day Frenzy

Which things in this picture are silly? It's up to you!

# Make a Move

Mr. and Mrs. Melody want to move into a new house. Mr. Melody is a music teacher and goes to school five days a week. Mrs. Melody manages a music shop and works six days a week. Which house should they choose if they want to travel the fewest total miles to and from work each week?

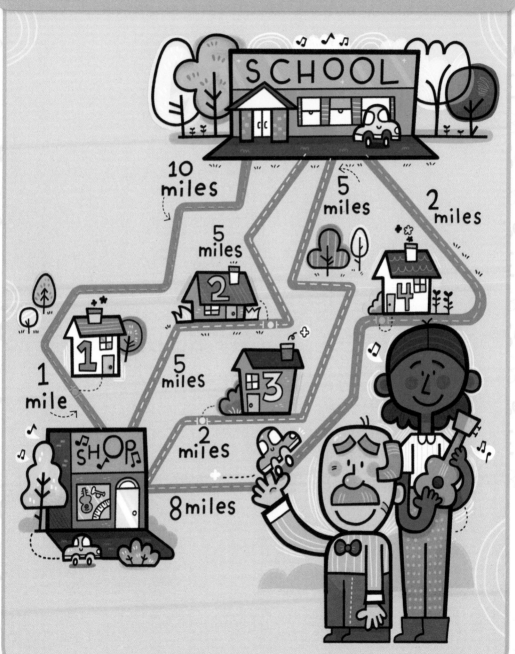

House 1 =
**112 MILES PER WEEK**

House 2 =
**110 MILES PER WEEK**

House 3 =
**74 MILES PER WEEK**

House 4 =
**116 MILES PER WEEK**

**Mr. and Mrs. Melody should move into House 3 to travel the fewest miles each week.**

# Just Sayin'

Give this person something to say. Then find the hidden
**CARROT**, **FLOWER**, **SPRING**, **TENNIS BALL**, and **WORM**.

Art by David Coulson

# Path Puzzle

These aliens need help finding their home planets. Draw a planet below each path, then follow the paths to see which planet belongs to which alien.

# Check . . . and Double Check

There are at least 18 differences between these two pictures.
How many can you find?

# Treasure Hunt

Can you find a path to the buried treasure? Start at the 5 in the top corner. You may move to a new box by adding 5 or subtracting 3. Move up, down, left, or right.

**START**

| 5 | 10 | 17 | 10 | 7 | 12 |
|---|---|---|---|---|---|
| 5 | 7 | 12 | 13 | 4 | 9 |
| 11 | 6 | 9 | 8 | 21 | 18 |
| 16 | 19 | 6 | 11 | 16 | 15 |
| 13 | 18 | 20 | 12 | 21 | 12 |
| 10 | 15 | 17 | 15 | 20 | 17 |

**FINISH**

Art by Dave Klug

# Hidden Pictures

Field trip time! Join this class on its outing to a lighthouse.
There are 10 hidden objects in the scene. How many can you spot?

saucepan

comb

eyeglasses

kite

scarf

arrow

banana

magnifying glass

turtle

rhinoceros

Art by Dave Klug

# Scrambled States

If you unscramble the letters on the light blue balloons, you can spell HAWAI'I. Which nine other states can you spell using each colored group of balloons?

●: _____

♡: _____

●: _____

♡: _____

●: _____

●: _____

●: _____

●: _____

●: _____

●: _____

Light blue: **HAWAI'I**
Dark blue: **UTAH**
Pink: **TEXAS**
Black: **OREGON**
Red: **IDAHO**
Purple: **ARIZONA**
White: **COLORADO**
Yellow: **ALASKA**
Green: **NEVADA**
Orange: **KANSAS**

# Emoji Matchup

Circle sets of four emojis together that have two bicycles and two motorcycles. One side of each square must touch a side of another square in the same set. You are done when all the squares are circled.

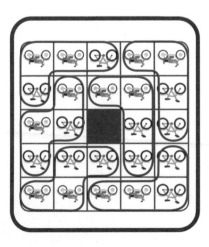

# Great Skate

It's a splendid day to go skating. There are five words (not pictures!) hidden in this scene. Can you find **BARK**, **CAKE**, **CANOE**, **HOLD**, and **WAIT**?

# Horse Smarts

These horses are all about numbers. And when they do math, the fun adds up! Where should each horse stand to make all the equations correct?

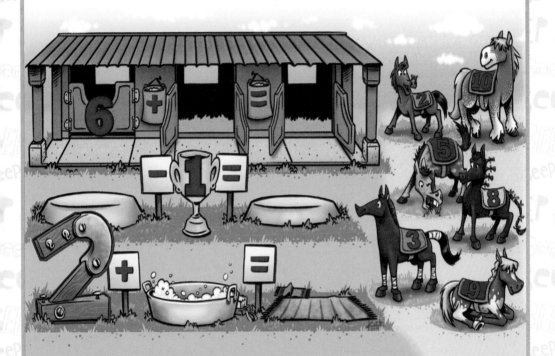

## Horse Ha-Ha's

**Where do horses go when they get sick?**
*The horse-pital*

**What is a horse's favorite state?**
*Maine*

**What do tired horses do at night?**
*They hit the hay.*

**What do you call a clumsy horse?**
*A Collides-dale*

Art by Kirk Wescom

6 + 2 = 8
10 − 1 = 9
2 + 3 = 5

# Car Code

Buckle up for some laughs. Use the car code to fill in the letters and finish the jokes below.

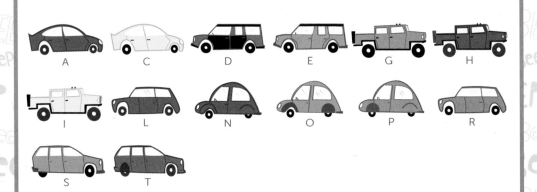

A    C    D    E    G    H

I    L    N    O    P    R

S    T

## What does a frog do when its car breaks down?

_____ _____ _____ _____ _____ _____ _____ _____ _____ _____ .

## Where do autos go swimming?

_____ _____ _____ _____ _____ _____ _____ _____ _____ _____

## What kind of cars do kittens ride in?

_____ _____ _____ - _____ _____ _____ _____ _____ _____

What does a frog do when its car breaks down?

**IT GETS TOAD.**

Where do autos go swimming?

**IN A CAR POOL**

What kind of cars do kittens ride in?

**CAT-ILLACS**

# Hide It!

Can you hide the paper airplane here in your own Hidden Pictures drawing?
We gave you some ideas in the sketches just below.

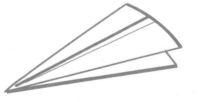

# Check . . . and Double Check

There are at least 10 differences between these two pictures.
How many can you find?

Art by Susan Miller

# Coasting Through

Are you ready for a rip-roaring ride?
Take this stomach-dropping coaster all the way from start to finish.

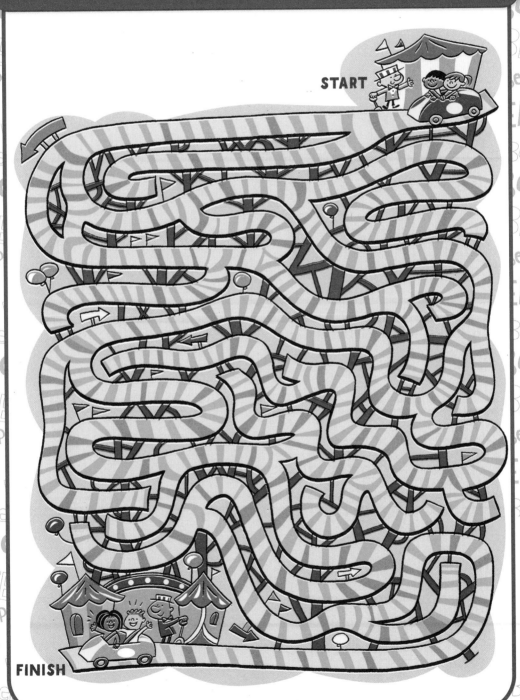

START

FINISH

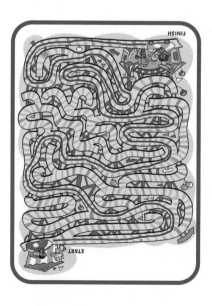

# Hidden Pictures

While these surfers catch some waves, can you catch the items hidden in this picture? There are 15 hidden objects in the scene. How many can you spot?

spoon

hat

ladder

spatula

teacup

dog bone

bat

mallet

paper airplane

flashlight

candy cane

tack

envelope

lollipop

slice of pizza

# A Message from the Past

Crossing the country in a covered wagon is no laughing matter, but that doesn't mean the pioneers didn't have a sense of humor. Decipher the coded riddle below by putting the last letter of each word first and the first letter last.

yhW did eht sioneerp srosc eht yountrc ni doverec sagonw?

eecausB yhet did ton tanw ot taiw yortf seary rof a nrait.

One type of wagon called the Conestoga held five tons of cargo.

**Knock, knock.**
*Who's there?*
**Wheel.**
*Wheel who?*
**Wheel be leaving in our wagon now.**
**Good-bye!**

Why did the pioneers cross the country in covered wagons?
**BECAUSE THEY DID NOT WANT TO WAIT FORTY YEARS FOR A TRAIN.**

# Tic Tac Skateboard

Each of these skateboards has something in common with the other two skateboards in the same row—across, down, and diagonally. For example, in the top row across, each skateboard has red wheels. Can you tell what's alike in each row?

# Skateboard Ha-Ha's

**How do you make a casserole?**

*Put it on a skateboard*

**What's the hardest thing about learning to skateboard?**

*The ground*

**What's black and white and very dangerous?**

*A cow on a skateboard*

Art by Paul Richer

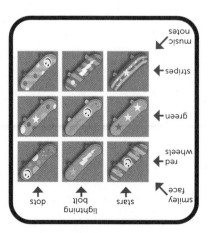

# Rush-Hour Rhymes

It's rush hour—but take all the time you need to find:
two matching dresses, plants, and lizards; a toad being towed;
a moose eating mousse; and a sail for sale.

# Plane Patterns

Each row of planes below has a number pattern. For instance, as you move from one plane to the next in the first row, the numbers should all go up by 3. But one plane in each row doesn't belong. Can you figure out which planes have the wrong numbers and what the correct numbers should be?

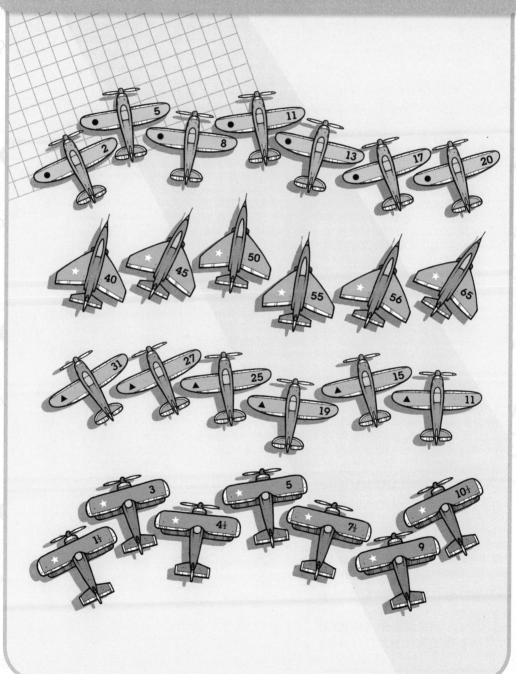

Row 1: **13 SHOULD BE 14 (COUNT UP BY 3.)**

Row 2: **56 SHOULD BE 60 (COUNT UP BY 5.)**

Row 3: **25 SHOULD BE 23 (COUNT DOWN BY 4.)**

Row 4: **5 SHOULD BE 6 (COUNT DOWN BY 1½.)**

# The Comics Page

These cartoons are missing something—speech balloons!
Can you match the speech balloons to the cartoons they belong to?

**1.**

**2.**

**3.**

**4.**

THIS IS ONE BUMPY RIDE.

**A.**

COULD YOU GIVE ME SOME DIRECTIONS? I THINK I LOST MY WAY.

**B.**

HAVE A BLAST ON YOUR TRIP.

**C.**

ROW, ROW, ROW YOUR GOAT...

**D.**

# Daring Dara

Dara loves a good adventure. Today, she's hang gliding over one of the
most amazing sights she's ever seen. What could it be?
Draw what you think Dara is gliding over.

# Check . . . and Double Check

There are at least 21 differences between these two pictures.
How many can you find?

Art by Kelly Kennedy

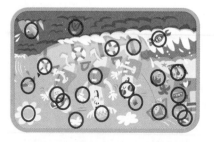

# Treehouse Trek

Here's a tree-rific challenge: Can you get from the ground to the top floor of this treehouse without waking any sleeping bats?

Art by Chuck Whelon

# Hidden Pictures

These astronauts are on a stellar journey!
There are 18 hidden objects in the scene. How many can you spot?

flashlight

sailboat

traffic light

dinosaur

fishhook

hockey stick

flag

cane

golf club

bell

bowl

fish

sock

ring

ladle

wedge of lemon

slice of pizza

needle

# Plane to See

Eighteen airplane names are jetting around this grid. They are hidden up, down, across, backward, and diagonally. How many can you land on?

## Word List

- CARGOMASTER
- CARIBOU
- CONSTELLATION
- EXPEDITOR
- FLYING BOXCAR
- HERCULES
- HUEY
- HUSKIE
- INVADER
- NIGHTINGALE
- PROVIDER
- SAMARITAN
- ~~SHOOTING STAR~~
- SKYMASTER
- SKYTRAIN
- STARLIFTER
- STRATOTANKER
- VALIANT

```
( S  H  O  O  T  I  N  G  S  T  A  R )  J
  N  F  N  I  G  H  T  I  N  G  A  L  E
  S  O  E  S  K  Y  M  A  S  T  E  R  D
  A  D  I  I  W  H  I  S  K  K  G  O  Q
  M  X  H  T  K  L  D  J  Y  C  A  T  P
  A  W  U  Y  A  S  K  Y  T  R  A  I  N
  R  U  E  V  R  L  U  V  X  H  T  D  U
  I  H  Y  P  I  B  L  H  J  M  K  E  O
  T  S  E  L  U  C  R  E  H  C  O  P  B
  A  S  T  A  R  L  I  F  T  E  R  X  I
  N  S  C  A  R  G  O  M  A  S  T  E  R
  C  R  E  D  I  V  O  R  P  G  N  M  A
  R  E  D  A  V  N  I  K  U  A  F  O  C
  F  L  Y  I  N  G  B  O  X  C  A  R  C
  R  E  K  N  A  T  O  T  A  R  T  S  O
```

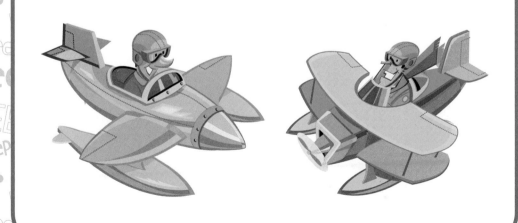

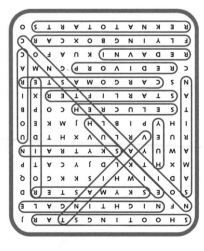

# Bicycle Q's

There's a lot to like about bikes.
Gear up for some cool bicycle activities below!

## Trail Treading

Can you help Evelyn get to the end of her mountain-bike trail?

START

FINISH

## Missing Vowels

**BCYCL** is the word *bicycle* with the vowels taken away. Can you figure out the names of these **BCYCL** parts?

_____

**HNDLBR**

_____

**SPKS**

_____

**WHLS**

_____

**BRKS**

_____

**GRS**

## Spin Cycle

Can you match each cycle to its description?

1. **Recumbent**

2. **Tandem**

3. **Unicycle**

4. **BMX**

5. **Rickshaw**

A. **Has only one wheel**

B. **Lets a rider lie back**

C. **Carries passengers in a cart**

D. **Used for racing and tricks**

E. **Designed for two riders**

# Trail Treading

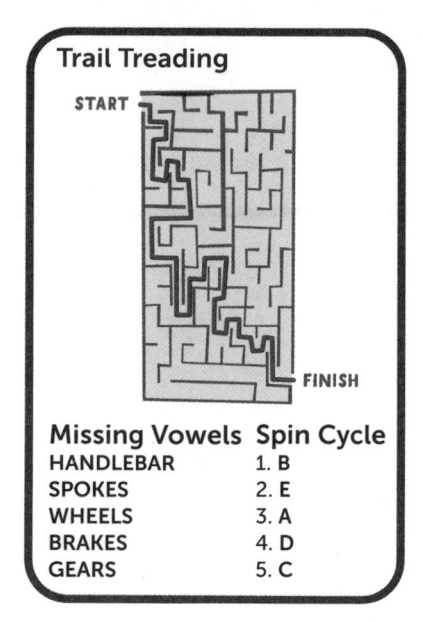

START

FINISH

## Missing Vowels

HANDLEBAR
SPOKES
WHEELS
BRAKES
GEARS

## Spin Cycle

1. B
2. E
3. A
4. D
5. C

# Fun in the Sun

Which things in this picture are silly? It's up to you!

EAT AT JOE'S

Art by Brian Michael Weaver

# Emoji Addition

Each vehicle emoji on this page has a value from 1 to 9. No two vehicles have the same value. Can you use the equations to figure out which number goes with which vehicle? The truck has the largest number and the motorcycle has the smallest number.

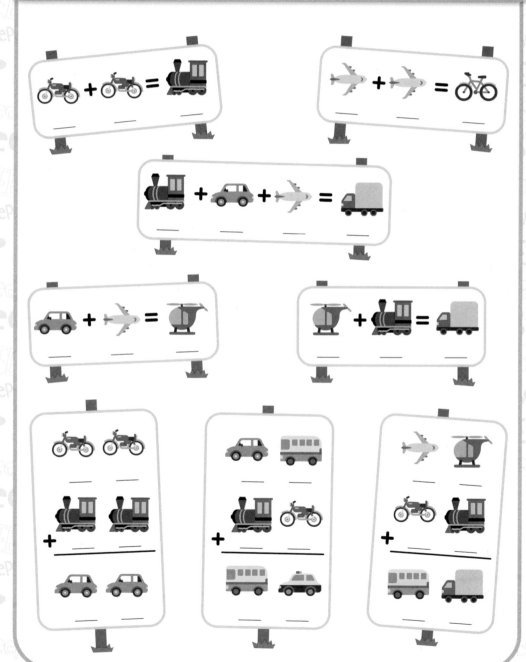

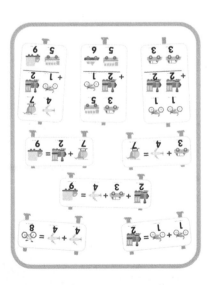

# Your Flight to _____.

PLACE

This is best played with a friend or family member. Without letting them read the story, ask for the words or phrases under the blanks. (For example, the first thing you'll ask for is a friend's first name.) After you've filled in all the blanks, read the story out loud.

Welcome to _____ Airlines. We're sorry, but your flight has
FRIEND'S FIRST NAME

been delayed _____ hours, and your luggage just took off for
BIG NUMBER

_____. Also, we won't be serving any food today, but all of our seat
FARAWAY COUNTRY

cushions are stuffed with _____. Our onboard TVs aren't working,
FOOD YOU DON'T LIKE

but the pilot will read from _____ during the flight over the plane's
YOUR FAVORITE BOOK

PA system.

We will begin boarding in _____ hours. If your socks have
BIG NUMBER

_____ on them and your shoes are _____, you will
NOUN (PLURAL)                                        ADJECTIVE

board first. If your favorite song is _____, you can sit by a window. If
YOUR FAVORITE SONG

that's not your favorite song, what's wrong with you? Passengers with small children or

extremely large _____ _____ should leave them
COLOR                    WILD ANIMAL (PLURAL)

in the cockpit with the pilot's babysitter. Oh! We do have some good news: Your flight

actually took off _____ minutes ago and will land on time!
SMALL NUMBER

Art by Mark Martin

# Float Along

The annual Homecoming Parade just rolled through town. This year's parade was filled with fantastic floats. What do you think the first-place float looked like? Draw it here.

# Check . . . and Double Check

There are at least 19 differences between these two pictures.
How many can you find?

Art by Kelly Kennedy

# Ka-yak Path

Follow the path so these yaks can get their kayaks in the lake!

START

FINISH

Art by Josh Cleland

# Hidden Pictures

A rabbit is causing a ruckus at this desert campsite! There are 12 hidden objects in the scene. How many can you spot?

ice-cream cone

banana

comb

hammer

light bulb

hot dog

yo-yo

mitten

fish

wedge of cheese

doughnut

canoe

# Ahoy!

Come sail away—or row, cruise, or float. Can you fit the 21 kinds of watercraft listed here into the grid? Bon voyage!

## WORD LIST

**4 LETTERS**

RAFT

SCOW

**5 LETTERS**

BARGE

CANOE

FERRY

KAYAK

SCULL

YACHT

**6 LETTERS**

DINGHY

JET SKI

**7 LETTERS**

GONDOLA

PONTOON

ROWBOAT

TUGBOAT

**8 LETTERS**

LIFEBOAT

SAILBOAT

**9 LETTERS**

CATAMARAN

HOUSEBOAT

SPEEDBOAT

STEAMBOAT

**10 LETTERS**

CRUISE SHIP

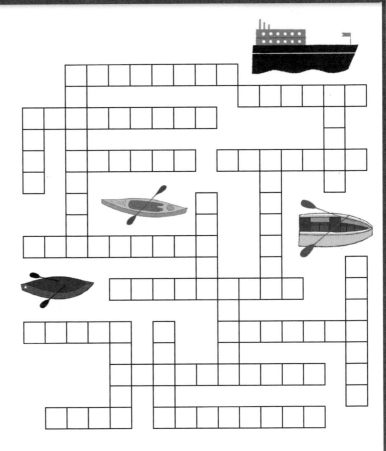

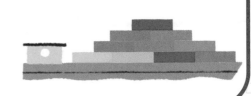

# Tic Tac Car

Each of these cars has something in common with the other two cars in the same row—across, down, and diagonally. For example, in the middle row across, all three cars have dogs. Can you tell what's alike in each row?

# Loopy Language

Can you match each language to its way of saying **CAR**?

1. \_\_\_ Catalan
2. \_\_\_ Italian
3. \_\_\_ Swahili
4. \_\_\_ Turkish
5. \_\_\_ Swedish
6. \_\_\_ French
7. \_\_\_ Indonesian

A. gli auto
B. araba
C. la voiture
D. mobil
E. bil
F. gari
G. cotxe

BEEP BEEP Beep Beep BEEP Beep BEEP Beep Beep

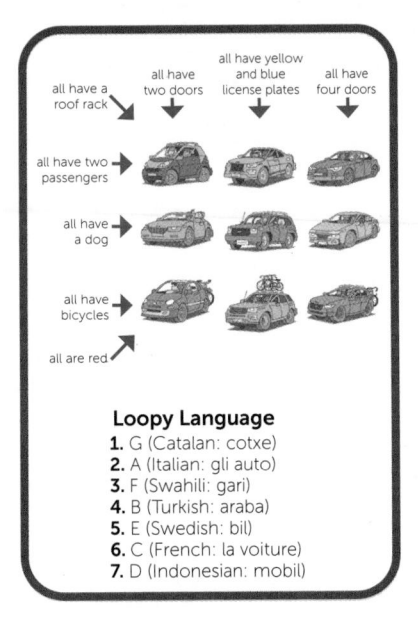

## Loopy Language

**1.** G (Catalan: cotxe)
**2.** A (Italian: gli auto)
**3.** F (Swahili: gari)
**4.** B (Turkish: araba)
**5.** E (Swedish: bil)
**6.** C (French: la voiture)
**7.** D (Indonesian: mobil)

# Animal Station

In the scene below, can you find at least one thing
that starts with each letter of the alphabet?

Art by Jennifer Harney

We found an **APPLE, BEAR, CAT, DOG, ELEPHANT, FOX, GIRAFFE, HEDGEHOG, IGUANA, JELLYFISH, KANGAROO, LION, MONKEY, NEST, OSTRICH, PEACOCK, QUAIL, RHINOCEROS, SQUIRREL, TICKET, UNICORN, VULTURE, WHEEL, XYLOPHONE, YARN,** and **ZEBRA**.

What else did you find?

# Gone Fishing

This fisherman had an interesting time at the lake today.
Can you figure out the order in which these scenes occurred?

# Just Sayin'

Give this snowman something to think. Then find the hidden **GOLF CLUB**, **PICKLE**, **SOCK**, **TOOTHBRUSH**, and **WISHBONE**.

Art by Felipe Galindo Gomez

# Sea This

This scuba diver has stumbled upon something exciting on her dive.
What do you think she found? Draw it here.

# Check . . . and Double Check

There are at least 20 differences between these pictures.
How many can you find?

# Navigation's a Go

Voyager Dusk is blasting off to Planet Zatz. To get there, the spaceship must first pass through Planet Zoop and the Moon of Zorka. Can you guide the spaceship to its destination while avoiding the black hole?

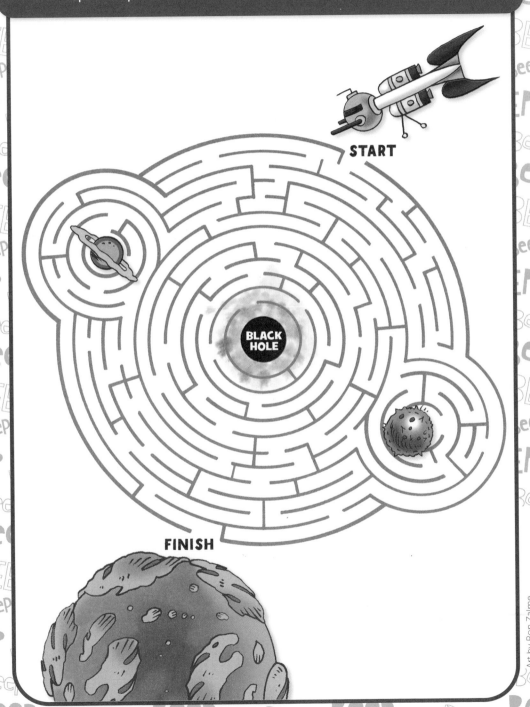

START

BLACK HOLE

FINISH

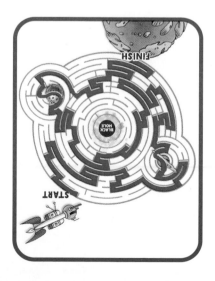

# Hidden Pictures

These fun-loving monsters are going with the flow on a river tubing trip.
There are 10 hidden objects in the scene. How many can you spot?

banana

slice of pie

boomerang

crescent moon

chili pepper

mug

spoon

yo-yo

pencil

stethoscope

# Riddle Sudoku

Fill in the squares so the six letters appear only once in each row, column, and 2 x 3 box. Then read the highlighted squares to find the answer to the riddle.

**Riddle:** Where do ants go on vacation?

Letters: **A F N R S T**

|   | S |   |   | R |   |
|---|---|---|---|---|---|
|   |   | T |   | F |   |
| N | F |   |   |   |   |
|   |   |   |   | A | F |
| S | N | F | R |   |   |
|   | A |   |   |   |   |

**Answer:** __ __ __ __ __ __ __

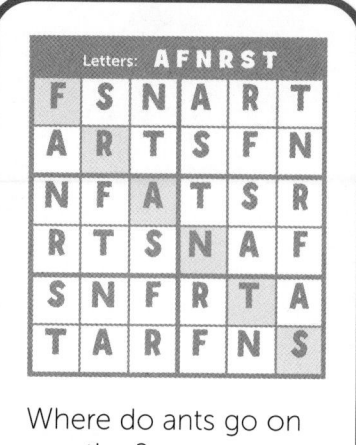

Where do ants go on vacation?

**FRANTS**

# Emoji Matchup

Circle sets of four emojis together that have one of each vehicle. One side of each square must touch a side of another square in the same set. You are done when all the squares are circled.

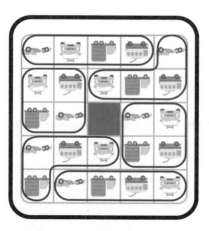

# Funny Fair

What things in this picture are silly? It's up to you!

Art by David Helton

# Map Mix-Up

People are flocking to Logicville for the big Summer Festival. Unfortunately, the new town maps were printed without labels on most of the buildings on Main Street. To help the lost tourists, read the clues below to figure out which building is which. Fill in the correct names on the map.

**1.** Archie's Arcade is one building south of the Sandwich Hut.

**2.** Izzy's Ice Cream is northeast of Archie's Arcade.

**3.** The Movie Palace is north of Sim's Sweets.

**4.** The T-Shirt Shack is one building south of Izzy's.

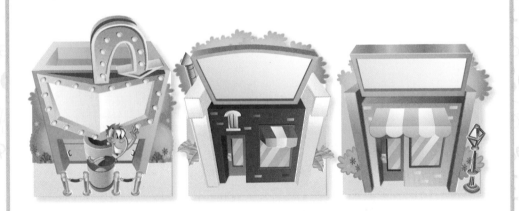

Art by Garry Colby    Puzzle by Sara Matson

| | | |
|---|---|---|
| Movie Palace | Sandwich Hut | Izzy's Ice Cream |
| Sim's Sweets | Archie's Arcade | T-Shirt Shack |

# Goose Code

Why did the goose cross the bridge? To find out, use the alphabet code to cross the puzzle bridge below. Start at the letter T on the bridge. To get the next code letter, count backwards (-) or forwards (+) in the alphabet the number of letters shown on the next stone. We did the first one for you: T – 5 = O. Keep following the arrows to crack the code.

A B C D E F G H I J K L M N O P Q R S T U V W X Y Z

-15   -22   +18
+8            -5
+7        +18   +1   +5
-3            -12
-11   +4            +1   +9
T   -5            -6   +8   -6

## WHY DID THE GOOSE CROSS THE BRIDGE?

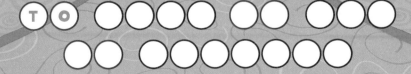

T O ○ ○ ○ ○ ○ ○ ○ ○ ○

○ ○ ○ ○ ○ ○ ○ ○

Art by Jim Steck

Why did the goose
cross the bridge?
**TO SHOW HE WAS NO
CHICKEN**

# Climb Confusion

These rock climbers got their ropes tangled. Can you set them straight?
Draw a rope partner at the bottom of each rope, and then follow each rope,
starting from the climber, to find out who his or her partner is.

Art by Jim Paillot

# Check . . . and Double Check

There are at least 21 differences between these two pictures.
How many can you find?

THE
SAVANNA
BIKE
RACE

THE
SAVANNA
BICYCLE
RACE

# Pack 'Em and Stack 'Em

It's time to get packing! Can you find a path through this stack of suitcases?

Art by Kelly Kennedy

# Hidden Pictures

*Whee!* These sledders are getting their glide on.
There are 12 hidden objects in the scene. How many can you spot?

comb

candy cane

toothbrush

crayon

feather

pen

slice of pie

magnet

open book

sock

banana

bell

Art by Dave Klug

# Liftoff!

There are 34 space terms inside the rocket. Circle all the words that you find. They can be vertical, horizontal, or diagonal. Write the leftover letters in order in the spaces below the rocket. They will give you an important message from mission control.

Mission control says, "_ _ _ _ _ _   _ _ _ _ !"

## WORD LIST

| | | | |
|---|---|---|---|
| APOGEE | CONTROL | MOMENTUM | RANGER |
| ARMS | COSMOS | MOONS | RE-ENTRY |
| ASTRONAUTS | FAIL-SAFE | MOUNTAIN | SALVO |
| ATOMIC | FORCE | NECK-WRENCHING | SPLASHDOWN |
| BOOSTERS | FUNDED | G-FORCES | SPACE DEBRIS |
| CAPE CANAVERAL | GUIDANCE SYSTEMS | NOSE CONE | THRUSTER |
| CAPSULES | LANDER | ORBIT | ZERO |
| CARGO | MANNED SPACESHIP | PERIGEE | ZOOM |
| CELESTIAL | MISSION | RAMJET | |

Art by Garry Colby

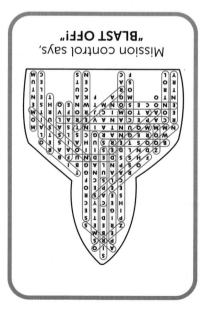

Mission control says,
**"BLAST OFF!"**

# Tic Tac Kite

Each of these kites has something in common with the other two kites in the same row—across, down, and diagonally. For example, in the first row across, all three are box kites. Can you tell what's alike in each row?

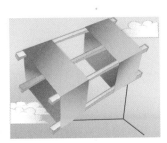

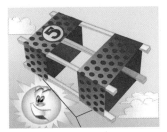

# Kite Ha-Ha's

**What does a kite say after a long day of flying?**

*"I'm winded!"*

**What material makes the best kites?**

*Flypaper*

**What do you call a kite's bad dream?**

*A kite-mare*

**Why was the kite so happy?**

*It had a string of good luck.*

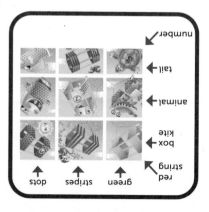

# Birds on Break

These feathered travelers are ready for the best vacation ever.
Join in the fun by finding the things listed below.

**GO!** Find a yo-yo, a banjo, and a bow.

**STOP!** Find flip-flops, gumdrops, a toy top, and a mop.

**QUACK!** Find a luggage rack and a salty snack.

Art by Kelly Kennedy

# First Flight

Joey, Haley, Talia, and Colin live in Oregon.
This summer, they will each fly on an airplane for the first time.
Use the clues to figure out where each friend is going.

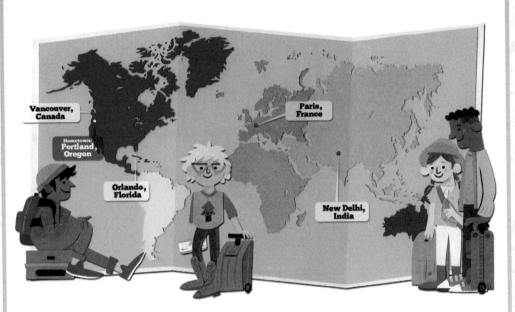

Use the chart to keep track of your answers. Put an **X** in each box that can't be true and an **O** in boxes that match.

|  | Vancouver, Canada | Paris, France | New Delhi, India | Orlando, Florida |
|---|---|---|---|---|
| Joey |  |  |  |  |
| Haley |  |  |  |  |
| Talia |  |  |  |  |
| Colin |  |  |  |  |

- Joey is flying out of the United States, but he will not cross an ocean.

- Haley will fly east across an ocean.

- Talia will travel farther east than Haley.

- Colin will travel farther than Joey, but he will not fly out of the United States.

Art by Jared Andrew Schorr

JOEY:
**VANCOUVER, CANADA**
HALEY:
**PARIS, FRANCE**
TALIA:
**NEW DELHI, INDIA**
COLIN:
**ORLANDO, FLORIDA**

# The Comics Page

These cartoons are missing something—speech balloons!
Can you match the speech balloons to the cartoons they belong to?

**1.**

**2.**

**3.**

**4.**

**A.**

**B.**

**C.**

**D.**

Art by Karen Sneide (sledders, skiers), Robert Leighton (skydiver in plane), and Felipe Galindo (cat skydiver)

1. **A**
2. **D**
3. **B**
4. **C**

# Hide It!

Can you hide the sailboat here in your own Hidden Pictures drawing? We gave you some ideas in the sketches just below.

 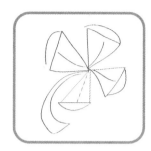

# Check . . . and Double Check

There are at least 18 differences between these two pictures.
How many can you find?

# Golfing Goats

Garin the Goat lost his golf ball.
Can you help him find a path through the golf course to find it?

START

FINISH

Art by Merrill Rainey

# Hidden Pictures

Let's play hide-and-seek with the hikers at this creek! There are 12 hidden objects in the scene. How many can you spot?

hot dog
carrot
hat
teacup
tent
artist's brush

ice-cream bar
leaf
muffin
horseshoe
sock
ladder

# Firefly Race

What do fireflies say at the start of a race? To find out, follow the directions below. Each sentence will tell you where one letter is in the grid. Once you've found it, write it in the correct space below the riddle.

1. This letter is between a **G** and an **O**.
2. This letter is the first consonant in the top row.
3. Find the letter directly below the **Q**.
4. This letter appears twice in the third row down.
5. This letter is right above the letter **V**.
6. Find this letter in the center of the second row.
7. Look to the left of the **V** for this letter.
8. This letter appears in two of the four corners.
9. This letter appears side by side in the same row.
10. Look for this letter directly above the **B**.
11. Count two above an **M** for this letter.
12. This letter is between two **A**'s.

| A | E | T | W | C | L | E |
| C | L | K | S | E | S | D |
| N | E | O | M | O | Q | W |
| L | V | R | R | H | Y | F |
| I | P | G | A | O | S | D |
| E | L | A | G | A | L | B |

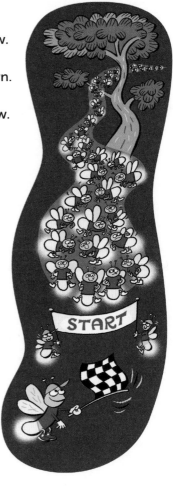

## What do fireflies say at the start of a race?

___ ___ **A** ___ ___ , ___ ___ ___ , ___ ___ ___ ___ !
9   5   1   10  3      6   8   2      12  7   4   11

Art by Kelly Kennedy

What do fireflies say at the start of a race?
**READY, SET, GLOW!**

# Skate Q's

Can't wait to skate? Lace up and complete the skating activities below.

## Get Rolling

Katie is racing to the finish line. Which place will she get?

## Hockey or Figure

Some of these terms come from **ice hockey** and others from **figure skating**. Can you figure out which belong to which sport?

| | H | F |
|---|---|---|
| SLAP SHOT | H | F |
| DOUBLE AXEL | H | F |
| ICING | H | F |
| TOE JUMP | H | F |
| LUTZ | H | F |
| FACEOFF | H | F |
| HAT TRICK | H | F |
| SALCHOW | H | F |
| DEATH SPIRAL | H | F |
| POWER PLAY | H | F |

## Trick or Not?

Each pair of terms has one inline skate trick and one faker. Can you tell which terms are the real tricks?

**Back Flip or Front Trip**

**Swing Set or Front Slide**

**Royale Grind or Rye Grinder**

**Mute Grab or Jute Bag**

**Grape Juice or Grapevine**

**Barrel Roll or Monkey Barrel**

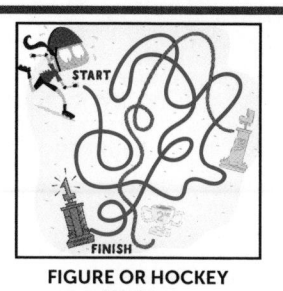

**FIGURE OR HOCKEY**
Hockey:
**SLAP SHOT, ICING, FACEOFF, HAT TRICK, POWER PLAY**

Figure Skating:
**DOUBLE AXEL, TOE JUMP, LUTZ, SALCHOW, DEATH SPIRAL**

**TRICK OR NOT**
The real tricks are:
**BACK FLIP, FRONT SLIDE, ROYALE GRIND, MUTE GRAB, GRAPEVINE, BARREL ROLL**

# Silly City

Which things in this picture are silly? It's up to you!

Art by David Arumi

# Beach Day

Gullbert had a busy day at the beach.
Can you figure out the order in which these scenes occurred?

# Race to the _____!

This is best played with a friend or family member. Without letting them read the story, ask for the words or phrases under the blanks. (For example, the first thing you'll ask for is a big number.) After you've filled in all the blanks, read the story out loud.

Good afternoon! This is the World Sledding Finals, where the winner gets

_____ extra-large _____ left-hand mittens! The red team is
BIG NUMBER              COLOR YOU DON'T LIKE

from Lower _____ Land. The blue team is from Upper _____ania, and
         VEGETABLE                         FRUIT

the green team is from Inner Western _____onia. But the green team just
                             YOUR FIRST NAME

canceled! They ate way too much _____ during the pre-race _____
                      DESSERT                          -ING VERB

party.

    Now to the action! The teams take off down Grand Squashed _____
                                                          INSECT

Hill. They're going fast! Watch out for that giant _____ snow sculpture!
                                      SMALL HOUSEHOLD PET

The red team is ahead, but wait . . . they're stopping and getting off the sled to dance

to _____! The blue team speeds past and takes the lead. Oh, no!
      YOUR FAVORITE SONG

Their sled is turning sideways, and the team is _____! That wasn't a pretty
                                         -ING VERB

_____. Now look at this! Here comes the green team after all! Their jackets are
    NOUN

made entirely of _____ feathers, so they're really flying now. It's going to
                   BIRD

be close! And the green team wins! What a race! It's just a shame there was no snow

on the ground.

Art by Pat Moriarity

# Daring Dara

What is Daring Dara jumping over now? A 20-layer cake?
A towering sandcastle? A grizzly bear on stilts? Use your imagination
and draw what you think Dara is about to soar over.

# Check . . . and Double Check

There are at least 17 differences between these two pictures.
How many can you find?

Art by Josh Cleland

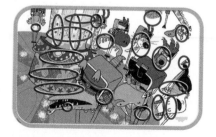

# Bull's-Eye

This parachuter is floating to earth.
Can you help him land safely right on target?

START

FINISH

Art by Jim Steck

# Hidden Pictures

A prankster alien has got its friends thinking an Earthling is running around their planet! There are 15 hidden objects in the scene. How many can you spot?

slice of pie · peanut · ice-cream cone · cotton candy · cookie · boomerang · kazoo · yo-yo · toy top · cactus · plunger · dog bone · canoe · wedge of cheese · lollipop

# Compass Code

How good is your sense of direction? To answer the riddle below, start at the North (N) circle. Then move in the directions listed and write the letters you find in the correct spaces. Get cracking before the sun goes down!

**Where's the best place to eat while hiking?**

Where there's

1. S 1    **A**

2. SE 2    ___

3. W 3    ___

4. NW 1    ___

5. S 3    ___

6. NE 3    ___

7. W 1    ___

8. S 2    ___

9. N 1    ___

10. SE 2    ___

11. W 3    ___

12. N 1    ___

13. E 2    ___

14. NW 2    ___

Art by Gary LaCoste

Where's the best place
to eat while hiking?

Where there's **A FORK IN
THE ROAD**

# Tic Tac Superhero

Each of these superheroes has something in common with the other two superheroes in the same row—across, down, and diagonally. For example, in the bottom row across, all three superheroes are wearing masks. Can you tell what's alike in each row?

# Superhero Ha-Ha's

**Why did the superhero save the pickle?**

*Because he wanted to eat it later.*

**Where do superheroes shop?**

*At the supermarket*

**What's the difference between a superhero and a fly?**

*A superhero can fly, but a fly can't superhero.*

**What do you call a computer superhero?**

*A screen saver*

Art by Dave Clegg

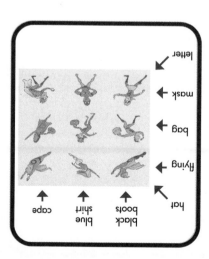

# Lake Escape

These vacationers are making a splash at the lake. There are six words (not pictures!) hidden in the scene. Can you find **LOOK**, **MATH**, **MINUTE**, **PINECONE**, **WHITE**, and **WORM**?

Art by Dave Klug

# Emoji Equations

Each vehicle emoji on this page goes with one number. No two emojis have the same number. Can you figure out which number goes with each emoji? The number 7 goes with the plane emoji. Use the equations to figure out the rest.

**A** 🚗 + 🚲 = **12**    🚗 − 🚲 = **6**
___ ___              ___ ___

**B** 🚕 + ✈️ = **17**    🚕 − ✈️ = **3**
___ 7               ___ 7

**C** 🚜 + 🚑 = **14**    🚜 − 🚑 = **2**
___ ___              ___ ___

**D** 🚙 + 🚁 = **20**    🚙 − 🚁 = **12**
___ ___              ___ ___

**E** 🚜 + 🚌 = **13**    🚜 − 🚌 = **3**
___ ___              ___ ___

**F** 🏍️ + ✈️ = **18**    🏍️ − ✈️ = **4**
___ 7               ___ 7

Art by Getty

A   🚗 + 🚲 = 12    🚗 − 🚲 = 6
   9    3       9    3

B   🚗 + ✈ = 17    🚗 − ✈ = 3
   10    7      10    7

C   🚙 + 🚑 = 14    🚙 − 🚑 = 2
   8    6       8    6

D   🚐 + 🚜 = 20    🚐 − 🚜 = 12
   16    4      16    4

E   🚙 + 🚌 = 13    🚙 − 🚌 = 3
   8    5       8    5

F   🏍 + ✈ = 18    🏍 − ✈ = 4
   11    7      11    7

# Just Sayin'

Give this swimmer something to say. Then find the hidden **BAT**, **ENVELOPE**, **FORK**, **ICE-CREAM CONE**, and **SLICE OF PIZZA**.

Art by Felipe Galindo Gomez

# Road Trip!

The Museum of the Silly is coming up in a few miles!
What do you think its billboard looks like? Draw it here.

# Check . . . and Double Check

There are at least 14 differences between these two pictures.
How many can you find?

# Go Team!

Help the Typhoon soccer team get their bus to the stadium by following the path from START to FINISH. Keep an eye out for the one-way streets!

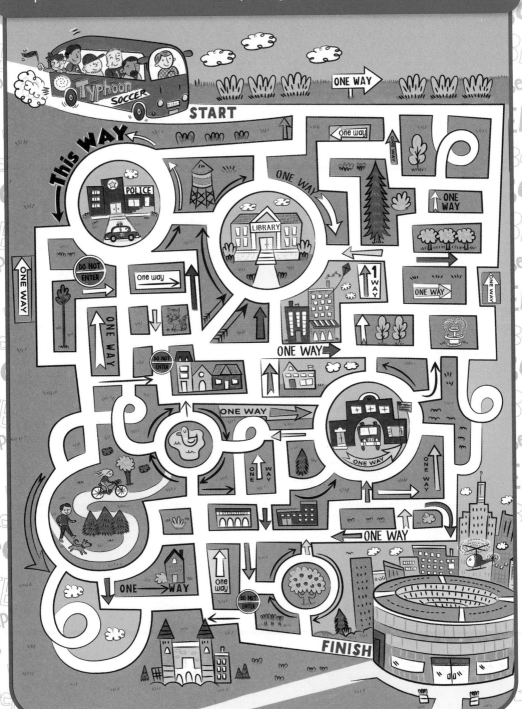

# Hidden Pictures

*Canoe* believe how much fun this family is having on their paddling trip?!
There are 12 hidden objects in the scene. How many can you spot?

hanger     scarf     banana     hammer     baseball bat

ladle     ring     glove     sock     paper clip     kite     bottle

# Giddyap!

Thirty-six horse and pony breeds from around the world are trotting through this grid. They are hidden up, down, across, backward, and diagonally. How many can you round up?

```
C L Y D E S D A L E L A O F T M
A P N A I R E V O N A H W S H G
M M U S T A N G L O K A I H O N
P P A L O M I N O Q L L P I R I
O F S R Q U A R T E R A N R O K
L F A O E I L F R O S Q N E U L
I O N Q B T T C G O R G A D G A
N U F A N C A A F I G I I N H W
A T R I O O I I L R E K N A B E
I A A L O T N I P A M P A L R E
G P T N T O Y B P O N Y B E E S
L D E A P P A L O O S A L N D S
E E L W A L K A L O O S A I N E
B R L I P I Z Z A N E I G H A N
W M O R G A N E K O N I K R L N
H J A N O T E R B R U M B Y T E
O I R I S H D R A U G H T P U T
A T R U S S I A N D O N E B J D
```

## Word List

ALBANIAN ~~ALBANIAN~~
ALTAI
APPALOOSA
ARABIAN
BANKER
BELGIAN
BLAZER
BRETON
BRUMBY
CAMPOLINA
CLYDESDALE

FOUTA
HANOVERIAN
IRISH DRAUGHT
JUTLAND
KONIK
LIPIZZAN
LOKAI
MORGAN
MUSTANG
PAINT
PALOMINO
PAMPA
PASA FINO

PINTO
QUARTER
RHINELANDER
RUSSIAN DON
SAN FRATELLO
SHIRE
TENNESSEE
  WALKING
THOROUGHBRED
TORI
WALER
WALKALOOSA
YILI

Art by Bob Ostrom

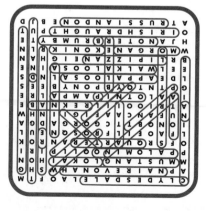

# Emoji Matchup

Circle sets of three emojis together that have one car of each color. One side of each square must touch a side of another square in the same set. You are done when all the squares are circled.

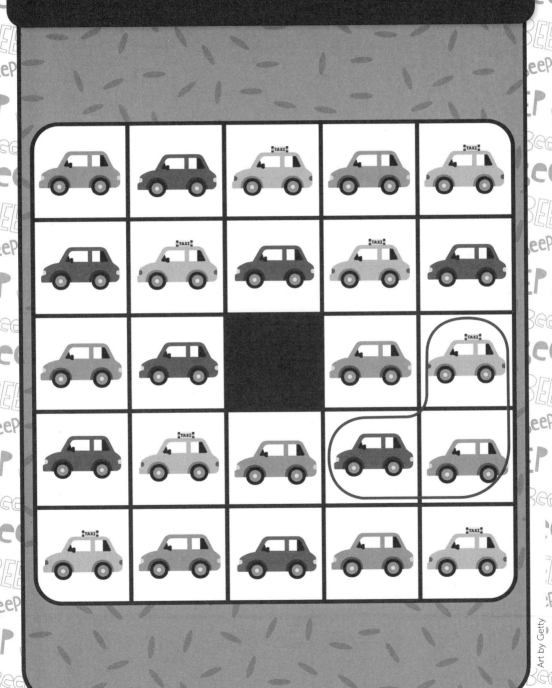

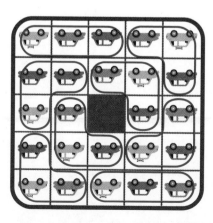

# Pedal Power

It's the perfect fall day for a bike ride. There are six words (not pictures!) hidden in the scene below. Can you find **BIKE**, **FALL**, **HELMET**, **OCTOBER**, **ORANGE**, and **WINDY**?

Art by Kelly Kennedy

# Skateboard Logic

Using the clues below, can you figure out what color skateboard each customer bought and how much each spent?

Use the chart to keep track of your answers. Put an **X** in each box that can't be true and an **O** in boxes that match.

|  | Dillon | Andrew | Anna |
|---|---|---|---|
| Yellow |  |  |  |
| Green |  |  |  |
| Orange |  |  |  |
| $60 |  |  |  |
| $70 |  |  |  |
| $80 |  |  |  |

- Anna spent $20 less than Dillon and $10 less than Andrew.

- Andrew doesn't like yellow.

- Dillon gave the cashier $100 and got $20 back in change when he bought his green skateboard.

Dillon: green, $80

Andrew: orange, $70

Anna: yellow, $60

# Hide It!

Can you hide the boomerang here in your own Hidden Pictures drawing?
We gave you some ideas in the sketches just below.

# Check . . . and Double Check

There are at least 17 differences between these two pictures.
How many can you find?

Art by Brian Michael Weaver

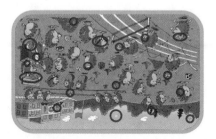

# Race, Car!

Can you help Racer Rex reach the FINISH line?

START

FINISH

Art by Mike Moran

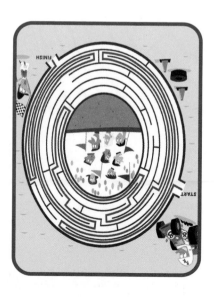

# Hidden Pictures

Let's go fly a kite! There are 14 hidden objects in the scene.
How many can you spot?

rake

sock

megaphone

seashell

caterpillar

envelope

banana

fishhook

fish

bell

slice of pizza

crescent moon

feather

necktie

Art by Daryll Collins

# Riddle Sudoku

Fill in the squares so the six letters appear only once in each row, column, and 2 x 3 box. Then read the highlighted squares to find the answer to the riddle.

**Riddle:** What only starts to work after it's fired?

**Letters: O T E R C K**

|   |   |   |   |   |   |
|---|---|---|---|---|---|
|   | K |   | E |   |   |
| C |   |   |   |   |   |
|   | R |   | T | O |   |
|   | E | O |   | R |   |
|   |   |   |   |   | R |
|   |   | R |   | K |   |

**Answer: A** _ _ _ _ _ _ _

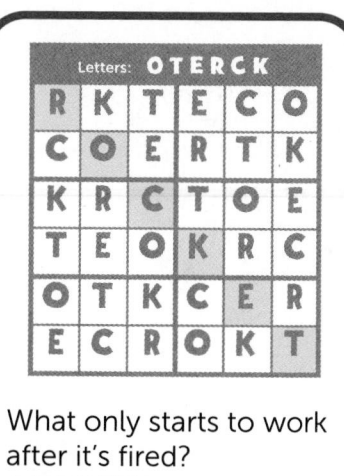

| Letters: | O | T | E | R | C | K |
|---|---|---|---|---|---|---|
| R | K | T | E | C | O |
| C | O | E | R | T | K |
| K | R | C | T | O | E |
| T | E | O | K | R | C |
| O | T | K | C | E | R |
| E | C | R | O | K | T |

What only starts to work after it's fired?
**A ROCKET**

# Kooky Kayaks

Which things in this picture are silly? It's up to you!

Art by David Helton

# The Comics Page

These cartoons are missing something—speech balloons! Can you match the speech balloons to the cartoons they belong to?

**1.**

**2.**

**3.**

**4.**

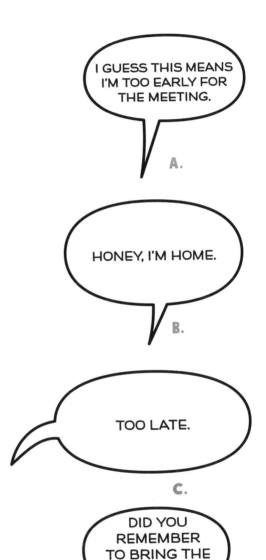

I GUESS THIS MEANS I'M TOO EARLY FOR THE MEETING.

**A.**

HONEY, I'M HOME.

**B.**

TOO LATE.

**C.**

DID YOU REMEMBER TO BRING THE ZORKULATOR?

**D.**

# Tropical Treat

An explorer rowed to a mysterious island. He can't believe what he found there! What do you think it is? Draw it here.

# Check . . . and Double Check

There are at least 16 differences between these two pictures.
How many can you find?

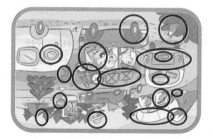

# Snow Go!

You won't be snow "bored" if you find the clear path to the FINISH flag.
If you run into a black line, you're going the wrong way!

START

FINISH

Art by R. Michael Palan

Use these stickers to mark your favorite on-the-go puzzles!

Highlights